Teddy's Train

A

LUCIA TOMAS **VICKY GIL**

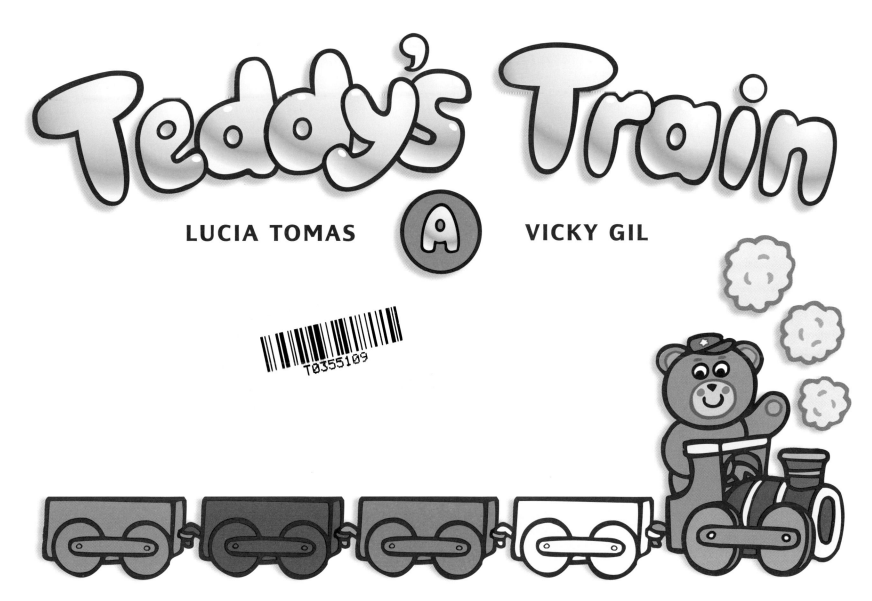

T0355109

Illustrations by Sonia Canals   Songs by Peter Hayward

OXFORD
UNIVERSITY PRESS

The following songs are introduced on this page:
- Hello
- Train's coming!
- Goodbye

Hello

Hello, hello.
Hello, everyone.
Hello, hello.
Hello, everyone.
Hello, hello.
Hello, everyone.
Hello, hello.
Hello, everyone.

Hello, children.
Hello, Teddy.
Hello, children.
Hello, Teddy.
Hello, children.
Hello, Teddy.
Hello, hello.
Hello, everyone.

Hello, hello.
Hello, everyone.
Hello, hello.
Hello, everyone.
Hello, hello.
Hello, everyone.
Hello, hello.
Hello, everyone.

Train's coming!

Train's coming! Train's coming!
Teddy's train's coming down the line.
Train's coming! Train's coming!
Coming down the line.

Train's coming! Train's coming!
Teddy's train's coming in on time.
Train's coming! Train's coming!
Coming in on time.

Chuff-a-chuff-a-chuff-chuff, clickety-clack,
Chuff-a-chuff-a-chuff-chuff, clackety-click,
Chuff-a-chuff-a-chuff-chuff, clickety-clack,
Shake, rattle, and roll.

Chuff-a-chuff-a-chuff-chuff, clickety-clack,
Chuff-a-chuff-a-chuff-chuff, clackety-click,
Chuff-a-chuff-a-chuff-chuff, clickety-clack,
Shake, rattle, and roll.

Goodbye

Goodbye, goodbye.
Goodbye, everyone.
Goodbye, goodbye.
Goodbye, everyone.
Goodbye, goodbye.
Goodbye, everyone.
Goodbye, goodbye.
Goodbye, everyone.

Goodbye, children.
Goodbye, Teddy.
Goodbye, children.
Goodbye, Teddy.
Goodbye, children.
Goodbye, Teddy.
Goodbye, goodbye.
Goodbye, everyone.

Goodbye, goodbye.
Goodbye, everyone.
Goodbye, goodbye.
Goodbye, everyone.
Goodbye, goodbye.
Goodbye, everyone.
Goodbye, goodbye.
Goodbye, everyone.

Lesson 1   Draw a picture of Teddy.
Lesson 2   Colour the train.
Lesson 3   Draw yourself next to Teddy.

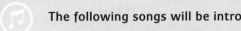

The following songs will be introduced in this unit:
- Look at the wagons (introduced on this page)
- Teddy's asleep (introduced on page 3)
- Teddy says (introduced on page 4)

Look at the wagons

Look at the wagons, the wagons, the wagons.
What's in the wagons, the wagons today?
Look at the wagons, the wagons, the wagons.
What's in the wagons, the wagons today?

What's in the yellow wagon?
A book!
Choo-choo, chuff-a-chuff

What's in the blue wagon?
A bag!
Choo-choo, chuff-a-chuff

What's in the red wagon?
A chair!
Choo-choo, chuff-a-chuff

What's in the green wagon?
A table!
Choo-choo, chuff-a-chuff

Choo, choo, chuff-a-chuff, chuff-a-chuff, chuff-a-chuff.
Choo, choo, chuff-a-chuff, chuff-a-chuff, chuff.
Choo, choo, chuff-a-chuff, chuff-a-chuff, chuff-a-chuff.
Choo, choo, chuff-a-chuff, chuff-a-chuff, chuff.

Choo, choo, chuff-a-chuff, chuff-a-chuff, chuff-a-chuff.
Choo, choo, chuff-a-chuff, chuff-a-chuff, chuff.
Choo, choo, chuff-a-chuff, chuff-a-chuff, chuff-a-chuff.
Choo, choo, chuff-a-chuff, chuff-a-chuff, chuff.

Teddy's asleep

Time to stop talking, time to sit down,
Hands on knees, quiet please,
Don't make a sound.

Teddy is sleeping, Teddy's asleep.
Settle down, not a sound,
Teddy's asleep.

Go to your table, go to your chair,
No one talk, slowly walk,
Have a rest there.

Teddy is sleeping, Teddy's asleep.
Settle down, not a sound,
Teddy's asleep.

Teddy says

Teddy says, 'Stand up'.
Teddy says, 'Sit down'.
Teddy says, 'Stand up'.
Teddy says, 'Turn around'.

Turn around,
Turn around, turn around,
Turn, turn, turn around.

Teddy says, 'Point up'.
Teddy says, 'Point down'.
Teddy says, 'Point up'.
Teddy says, 'Turn around'.

Turn around,
Turn around, turn around,
Turn, turn, turn around.

Teddy says, 'Point up'.
Teddy says, 'Sit down'.
Teddy says, 'Stand up'.
Teddy says, 'Turn around'.

Turn around,
Turn around, turn around,
Turn around,
Turn around, turn around...

Teddy says, 'Stop'.
Teddy says...
'Well done, everyone!'
'Hooray!'

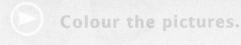

Colour the pictures.

Follow the paths and colour the pictures.

Colour the pictures to match the models.

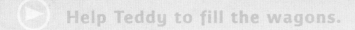

Help Teddy to fill the wagons.

The following song will be introduced in this unit:

- One, two, three (introduced on page 8)

One, two, three

One, two, three.
One, two, three.
Knock, knock, knock,
One, two, three.
Open the door and you will see,
Knock, knock, knock,
One, two, three,
Someone's at the door.

Knock, knock, knock,
Knock, knock, knock,
One, two, three,
One, two, three.
Knock, knock, knock,
Knock, knock, knock,
Someone's at the door.

Knock, knock, knock,
Knock, knock, knock,
One, two, three,
One, two, three.
Knock, knock, knock,
Knock, knock, knock,
Someone's at the door.

One, two, three.
One, two, three.
Knock, knock, knock,
One, two, three.
Open the window and you will see,
Knock, knock, knock,
One, two, three.
Someone's at the window.

Knock, knock, knock,
Knock, knock, knock,
One, two, three,
One, two, three.
Knock, knock, knock,
Knock, knock, knock,
Someone's at the window.

Knock, knock, knock,
Knock, knock, knock,
One, two, three,
One, two, three.
Knock, knock, knock,
Knock, knock, knock,
Someone's at the window.

Unit 2 At Teddy's house

Colour the pictures.

6

Colour the picture to match the model.

8

Draw yourself and Teddy. Stick your drawings behind the door or the windows.

Teddy's Train © Oxford University Press

Circle the right number of teddies.

10

 **Draw a picture on the TV.**

The following song will be introduced in this unit:

- At the swimming pool (introduced on page 13)

At the swimming pool

Shake your arm,
Shake your leg,
Shake your hand,
Shake your head.
Reach up high,
Touch the sky.
Can you see us
At the swimming pool?

Shake your arm,
Shake your leg,
Shake your hand,
Shake your head.
Reach up high,
Touch the sky.
Can you see us
At the swimming pool?

Splash, splash, splash. Wheee!
Splash, splash, splash. Wheee!
Splash, splash, splash. Wheee!
Splaaaaaaaaaaashhhhh!

Now jump in,
Now jump out,
Now jump down,
Now jump up.
Reach up high,
Touch the sky.
Can you see us
At the swimming pool?

Now jump in,
Now jump out,
Now jump down,
Now jump up.
Reach up high,
Touch the sky.
Can you see us
At the swimming pool?

Splash, splash, splash. Wheee!
Splash, splash, splash. Wheee!
Splash, splash, splash. Wheee!
Splaaaaaaaaaaashhhhh!
Splash, splash!

Colour the pictures.

Put the pictures in the right order to make a story.

Colour the pictures to match the model.

13

14

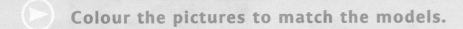

Colour the pictures to match the models.

Complete and colour the picture.

The following song will be introduced in this unit:

- Blow the balloon (introduced on page 18)

Blow the balloon

Blow, blow, blow the balloon.
Make it bigger, bigger and bigger.
Let's blow, blow, blow the balloon.
Ooof! Ooof! Ooof!

Squeeze, squeeze, squeeze the balloon.
Make it smaller, smaller and smaller.
Let's squeeze, squeeze, squeeze the balloon.
Bppp! Bppp! Bppp!

Blow, blow, blow the balloon.
Make it bigger, bigger and bigger.
Let's blow, blow, blow the balloon.
Ooof! Ooof! Ooof!

Squeeze, squeeze, squeeze the balloon.
Make it smaller, smaller and smaller.
Let's squeeze, squeeze, squeeze the balloon.
Bppp! Bppp! Bppp!

Blow, blow, blow the balloon.
Make it bigger, bigger and bigger.
Let's blow, blow, blow the balloon.

Ooof! Ooof! Ooof!
Ooof! Ooof! Ooof! Ooof!
Ooof! Ooof! Ooof! Ooof...
POP!

Colour the pictures.

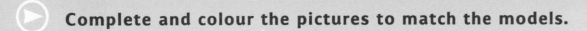

Complete and colour the pictures to match the models.

Complete and colour the pictures.

Colour the hats to match the clothes.

Teddy's Train © Oxford University Press

20

Complete the series.

The following song will be introduced in this unit:

- Woof says the dog (introduced on page 23)

Woof says the dog

Woof, woof, woof says the dog,
Woof says the dog,
Woof says the dog.
Woof, woof, woof says the dog.
Who will you be today?

Miaow, miaow, miaow says the cat,
Miaow says the cat,
Miaow says the cat.
Miaow, miaow, miaow says the cat.
Who will you be today?

Glug, glug, glug says the fish,
Glug says the fish,
Glug says the fish.
Glug, glug, glug says the fish.
Who will you be today?

Tweet, tweet, tweet says the bird,
Tweet says the bird,
Tweet says the bird.
Tweet, tweet, tweet says the bird.
Who will you be today?

Colour the pictures.

Help Teddy to find the bone.

Colour the pictures to match the models.

24

Follow the paths. Draw the right animal in the wagons.

Match the pictures. Colour them to match the models.

The following songs will be introduced in this unit:
- The picnic song (introduced on page 28)
- Saying goodbye (introduced on page 30)

The picnic song

Picnic, picnic,
We're going on a picnic.
Let's have fun,
There's food for everyone.

Banana, banana,
Peel the banana.
Yum, yum, yum,
It's going in my tum.

Doo-be-doo, ZIP!
Doo-be-doo, ZIP!
Doo-be-doo, doo-be-doo,
ZIP! ZIP! ZIP!
Doo-be-doo, ZIP!
Doo-be-doo, ZIP!
Doo-be-doo, doo-be-doo,
ZIP! ZIP! ZIP!

Picnic, picnic,
We're going on a picnic.
Let's have fun,
There's food for everyone.

Apple, apple,
Bite the apple.
Yum, yum, yum,
It's going in my tum.

Doo-be-doo, CRUNCH!
Doo-be-doo, CRUNCH!
Doo-be-doo, doo-be-doo,
CRUNCH! CRUNCH! CRUNCH!
Doo-be-doo, CRUNCH!
Doo-be-doo, CRUNCH!
Doo-be-doo, doo-be-doo,
CRUNCH! CRUNCH! CRUNCH!

Picnic, picnic,
We're going on a picnic.
Let's have fun,
There's food for everyone.

Sandwich, sandwich,
Chew the sandwich.
Yum, yum, yum,
It's going in my tum.

Doo-be-doo, CHOMP!
Doo-be-doo, CHOMP!
Doo-be-doo, doo-be-doo,
CHOMP! CHOMP! CHOMP!
Doo-be-doo, CHOMP!
Doo-be-doo, CHOMP!
Doo-be-doo, doo-be-doo,
CHOMP! CHOMP! CHOMP!

Picnic, picnic,
We're going on a picnic.
Let's have fun,
There's food for everyone.

Cake, cake,
Eat the cake.
Yum, yum, yum,
It's going in my tum.

Doo-be-doo, MUNCH!
Doo-be-doo, MUNCH!
Doo-be-doo, doo-be-doo,
MUNCH! MUNCH! MUNCH!
Doo-be-doo, MUNCH!
Doo-be-doo, MUNCH!
Doo-be-doo, doo-be-doo,
MUNCH! MUNCH! MUNCH!

Doo-be-doo, ZIP! CRUNCH! CHOMP! MUNCH!
Doo-be-doo, ZIP! CRUNCH! CHOMP! MUNCH!
Doo-be-doo, doo-be-doo,
YUM! YUM! YUM!

Saying goodbye

We're saying goodbye to Teddy's train.
Goodbye, goodbye, saying goodbye.
We're saying goodbye to Teddy's train.
Goodbye, goodbye, goodbye.

We're saying goodbye to Teddy's train.
Goodbye, goodbye, saying goodbye.
We're saying goodbye to Teddy's train.
Goodbye, goodbye, goodbye.

Unit 6 At a picnic

Colour the pictures.

27

Find the things to eat. Colour them.

Help Teddy to find the things to eat.

Complete the series.

Colour the pictures to match the models.

Christmas song

Ding, dong, ding, dong,
Ring the Christmas bells.
Ding, dong, ding, dong,
Ring the Christmas bells.

Wishing you a Happy Christmas,
Wishing you a Happy New Year.
Wishing you a Happy Christmas,
Wishing you a Happy New Year.

Ding, dong, ding, dong,
Ring the Christmas bells.
Ding, dong, ding, dong,
Ring the Christmas bells.

Wishing you a Happy Christmas,
Wishing you a Happy New Year.
Wishing you a Happy Christmas,
Wishing you a Happy New Year.

Ding, dong, ding, dong,
Ding, dong, ding, dong...
HAPPY CHRISTMAS EVERYONE!

Christmas

Draw a picture to make a card.

Easter

Easter,
Easter's here.
Easter,
Give a cheer.
Easter time, Easter time,
Easter time is here.
Bunnies hop,
Hop, hop, hop.
Easter time is here.

Easter,
Easter's here.
Easter,
Give a cheer.
Easter time, Easter time,
Easter time is here.
Bunnies hop,
Hop, hop, hop.
Fluffy chicks cheep,
Cheep, cheep, cheep.
Easter time is here.

Easter,
Easter's here.
Easter,
Give a cheer.
Easter time, Easter time,
Easter time is here.
Bunnies hop,
Hop, hop, hop.
Fluffy chicks cheep,
Cheep, cheep, cheep.
Easter eggs,
Yum, yum, yum...
Easter time is here.

Easter

Draw a picture to make a card.